THE 30-DAY SPEED
SONGWRITING CHALLENGE

THE 30-DAY SPEED SONGWRITING CHALLENGE

ED BELL

Bell, Ed
Book : The 30-Day Speed Songwriting Challenge

Library of Congress Control Number: 2019909930

ISBN 978-0-9981302-6-2 (Paperback edition)

Published September 2019
New York City

CONTENTS

Yep – You're Going to Write Fifteen Songs This Month i

Days 1–2: Chorus Lyric Starter 2

Days 3–4: Chord Progression Starter................6

Days 5–6: Title Starter 10

Days 7–8: Forbidden Love 14

Days 9–10: Word Cluster #1 18

Days 11–12: Off the Hook 22

Days 13–14: One-to-One....................26

Days 15–16: Get Happy....................30

Days 17–18: Word Cluster #2 34

Days 19–20: This Time It's Personal...............38

Days 21–22: The Response Challenge 42

Days 23–24: The Ballad Challenge..................46

Days 25–26: Title Remix 50

Days 27–28: The Farewell Challenge 54

Days 29–30: So Many Possibilities 58

...And Breathe – You Did It! 62

Coda: Five Surefire Ways of Beating W****r's B***k.......69

Appendix 1: Song Structure Cheatsheet.......................... 81

Appendix 2: One Effective Songwriting Process............. 85

Appendix 3: 107 Bonus Song Prompts 89

ABOUT THE SONG FOUNDRY

At The Song Foundry it's our mission to share great songwriting ideas with the world. At thesongfoundry.com we publish articles about songwriting, host free videos on various songwriting topics, and offer Skype songwriting coaching worldwide.

Connect with us online to find out more:

thesongfoundry.com

youtube.com/TheSongFoundry

facebook.com/TheSongFoundry

twitter.com/TheSongFoundry

ALSO AVAILABLE

The 30-Day Lyric Writing Challenge

The 30-Day Creativity Challenge

The 30-Day Music Writing Challenge

Find out more about all the 30-Day Challenges at
thesongfoundry.com/30-day-challenges

YEP – YOU'RE GOING TO WRITE FIFTEEN SONGS THIS MONTH

Hello – and welcome to *The 30-Day Speed Songwriting Challenge*, where you're going to spend the next month writing fifteen brand new songs.

Yep. That's not a typo. You're not hallucinating.

You're genuinely going to complete fifteen new songs in the next thirty days.

How? I'll explain.

Why? I'll explain that too.

Actually, let's start with why.

One of the hardest things about songwriting is getting started. That's true whether you're writing your first song or holding your first Grammy. The blank page is scary. It could be anything. It could be something you're not proud of. It could be something that leaves people disliking it – or worse, leaves people thinking 'meh'.

If you can relate, congratulations: it means you're human. It means you're normal.

It's completely normal to feel scared or nervous when you start a new song. But if there's one cure for fear, it's this: action.

Do something.

Try something.

Get the $&%! on with writing something. Anything.

Courage isn't about getting rid of fear. It's about overcoming it – feeling afraid but doing what you have to do anyway.

And oh boy, if you want to be creative, you have to learn to be courageous.

You have to be courageous enough to start, even when you don't know where you're going. You have to be courageous to keep going even when you're *still* not sure what you're doing, your big idea for this project has changed four times already and you're not sure how or when you'll get this project finished.

You have to find the courage to *do*, even when you don't feel like it. That's all there is to it.

And like virtually everything else, your ability to do that is like a muscle – the more you use it, the stronger it gets.

The more comfortable you get being uncomfortable – conquering your resistance and doing what you've got to do anyway – the better prepared you'll be for taking on bigger creative challenges in future.

And that, in short, is why *The 30-Day Speed Songwriting Challenge* exists – to help you take a hatchet to your comfort zone, to help you prove to yourself what you're capable of, and to help you overcome w****r's b***k for good.

And that's why you're going to write fifteen new songs over the next thirty days – to prove to yourself that you can write under pressure, to prove to yourself that you can make snap creative decisions and roll with whatever ideas you have, and to prove to yourself that it's always better to write something OK and improve it later than sit around writing nothing at all. (Because you definitely can't improve a blank page.)

Still, I'm not going to lie – writing fifteen new songs in thirty days is no small task. And while we're being honest, I'm not going to guarantee that every one of the fifteen songs you're about to write will be your best, most individual, most ground-breaking work. Because it doesn't work like that.

But by writing fifteen new songs in as little as a month you will see an incredible transformation not only in your ability to write, but in your ability to shut your inner critic up, your ability to be brave enough to try things out, and your ability to overcome self-doubt and just keep moving towards your songwriting goals.

At the end of this book – like in all of my 30-Day Challenges – we'll talk about how you can turn the material you created in this challenge into something more substantial and polished if you want to, but let me say it again: that's not the primary goal of this challenge.

If you end up with some great material – and let's face it, you probably will – great. But that's kind of a side effect of getting through this challenge.

Your most important goal in the next thirty days is to turn out fifteen competent, coherent songs, to prove to yourself that you can. To convince yourself that you're full of tons of great ideas – way more than you realize – but the only way to prove that is to get those ideas down on a page, on a screen or in a voicenote. To remind yourself that play and procrastination have their place in the creative process, but at the end of the day, good things come to those who write – often.

So that's why you're going to write fifteen songs this month.

Now let's talk about how.

Most of all, there's really only one ground rule when it comes to completing these challenges: write.

Write something.

Write anything.

Write now, think later. Just get it down – build, create and get those ideas out.

Each challenge begins with a specific stimulus or starting point – a lyric, a page full of words, an idea, a chord progression, something like that – to make that as easy as possible for you.

Each challenge challenges comes with at least a couple of paragraphs of tips or advice to help you hit the ground running. It's obviously up to you how seriously you want to take all of that – you might already have your own ideas and working methods – but as long as you roll with the challenge in front of you and do your thing with it, it's all good.

You can – and should – complete the challenges in whatever style or genre you like, with whatever combination of instruments and technology you've got, and with whatever prior songwriting knowledge and experience you have already.

All of the challenges are open-ended enough they'll work in any style with whatever you can bring to the table as a songwriter. So get ready to do what you already do, and take everything to the next level.

You can do the challenges solo if you're happy writing both music and lyrics, or you can work with a co-writer if you'd prefer that or need to schedule writing sessions with someone else to keep you on track throughout the thirty days. That's totally up to you. (You could even do the challenges once through solo and again with one or more co-writers if you like.)

I recommend you spread the challenges evenly across the thirty days – one every other day for the month. You could, of course, do them in less or more than thirty days, but if you can I recommend that you complete each challenge in one sitting. Like I said, that's no small task, but you'll probably get more from each challenge by doing it in one intensive burst, rather than spread out over two or more writing sessions. That's why I recommend alternating write days and rest days for thirty days.

In theory, you could spend as much or as little time as you like on each project. But honestly, spending eight to ten hours on each one wouldn't be much of a speed songwriting challenge and probably wouldn't help you out that much. That's why I strongly recommend you give yourself 60–90 minutes for each project – no exceptions.

I know, that's not a ton of time. But it's bang in the goldilocks zone: long enough to complete each challenge but short enough that there's no time for overthinking or umming and ahhing – which is definitely the technical term – to keep you, your fingers and your ideas moving.

So go ahead: come up with a plan for fifteen 90-minute slots over the next thirty days. Write it down somewhere. Then, like bacon to a cheap frying pan, make sure you stick to it.

That's because – like in all of my 30-Day Challenges – the key to getting to the end of this one is songwriting's most important C word, other than 'chorus': consistency. You have to show up consistently if you want to get the maximum benefits from these challenges.

That means starting consistently – sticking to your plan – but it also means finishing consistently – giving each 60–90-minute slot everything you've got. In these challenges, that means especially that you don't start letting your inner perfectionist get the better of you somewhere around Day 14, and you keep writing and try to get each project finished, no matter what.

Honestly, if you don't finish some days, but you give the 60–90 minutes your all, that's OK. Give yourself permission to have an off day or write less than your best work every now and then. Let yourself complete something that works for now and save worrying about filtering or editing what you write for some other time. (We'll talk more about how you can do that once you're done.)

If some days you finish a challenge with time to spare though, you can always go back and edit, polish or rewrite what you've got. But before you worry about any of that, it's important to focus on getting a complete first draft finished for each challenge, and only then thinking about making changes.

Again, you have free rein to complete each challenge in whatever style or genre and with whatever technology, instruments and/or voices you like. But whatever you do, I recommend you generally stick with simple versions of two of the most straightforward song forms: verse-chorus form and refrain form. Sometimes its fun to see how you can reinvent the wheel, but not when you only have 90 minutes to do it.

I've also given you a ton of bonus material in the back of the book which you can consult either before you start or as you work through the challenges.

First up is a bonus chapter I've glamorized as the book's 'Coda', which outlines five specific and powerful techniques for busting w****r's b***k. While I wish I could tell you busting every resistance to writing you'll ever experience is as simple as reading nine pages of ideas, it doesn't work like that. But still, if you get particularly stuck at any point in the challenges – as well as in real life – the techniques in this section will definitely come in useful. So this section is absolutely worth checking out before you get started on the challenges. (Or before you start every new challenge if you need it.)

After that there are three short appendixes:

Appendix 1 summarizes the two song forms I recommend you use in these challenges if you need a quick refresher.

Appendix 2 outlines one simple but effective process you can use for crafting songs from scratch, based on the process I outline in my book *How to Write a Song (Even If You've Never Written One Before and You Think You Suck)*.

Then finally, Appendix 3 contains 107 specific song prompts in case you need them for a couple of the challenges or just want to use them for writing other songs in the future.

And that's about it. That's pretty much everything you need to know to get started.

Other than that, now is a great time to give your inner critic one final reminder that it's not welcome anywhere near here for the next thirty days – because there's writing to be done.

So let's get cracking.

"That's how you accomplish things in life. You don't sit around talking about it; you just do it. If you really want to go far in life, you do things that are hard and that you think you can't do."

MARTIN BECKNER

[DAYS 1–2]
CHORUS LYRIC
STARTER

[DAYS 1–2]

CHORUS LYRIC STARTER

"Don't judge it. Just write it. Don't judge it.
It's not for you to judge it."
PHILIP ROTH

Alrighty, for your first challenge I'm going to give you a generous head start. I've written a complete chorus lyric, and it's up to you to build a complete song around it.

As I said in the Introduction, while in these challenges you can write in any genre or style, I recommend you keep each song structure simple. In fact, for your first challenge I recommend you aim for a Verse–Chorus–Verse–Chorus structure, with 8 lines and 16 measures for each section.

> **Why it matters:** The key to all of these challenges is to get your ideas down without pausing to judge or edit yourself. In today's challenge, you've already got a nice head start – you just have to keep building from there.

DAYS 1–2 CHALLENGE

 60–90 mins

Build a complete song given this chorus lyric:

ONE OF A KIND

You're one of a kind,

Ain't no denyin'.

I couldn't replace ya,

Ain't no point tryin'.

You stole my heart and my soul

And my goddamn mind.

Cuz there ain't nobody like you,

You're one of a kind.

Start working on this challenge any place you like, but if you're not sure, a great place to start is by finding a melody and chords to match this lyric, then a groove underneath that seems to support what it's saying. (You're welcome to make minor changes to the lyric if it helps.) From there you can start thinking about the verses – what they're going to say and what they're going to sound like.

Now is also a good time to take a step back and decide what this song is about overall – who is singing, who they're singing to, and why they're sharing this song's message – before you write the rest of the song. (You can check Appendix 2 for more guidance on this.)

[DAYS 3–4]
CHORD
PROGRESSION
STARTER

[DAYS 3–4]

CHORD PROGRESSION STARTER

"I never judge my own songwriting. It's just my heart.
What's there to judge about your own heart?"
BANKS

One of the best ways to get into a new song is to start with a chord progression – it gives you a solid base and structure to build everything else on top of.

So that's what you're going to do in today's challenge – I've written verse and chorus chord progressions for you, then it's up to you to write the rest of the song using them.

Like before, you'll want to spend some time thinking about what the song is about – what story or concept it explores – before you dive into any serious writing.

Why it matters: A solid chord progression is a great foundation for an entire song – so being able to build grooves, melodies and lyrics around them is an essential songwriting skill.

DAYS 3–4 CHALLENGE

 60–90 mins

Build a complete song out of these verse and chorus chord progressions:

VERSE

Am		G		F			G	
Am		G		F			G	
Am		G/B		C		Am		
Dm		F		G				

CHORUS

Am		F		C			G/B	
Am		F		C			G/B	
Am		F		C		C/E		
F				C				

Start building musically from wherever you like – with a groove, vocal melody, rhythm, anything. Once you have a song idea or story that suits the music you've created, you can then try crafting a full lyric. In this challenge, I recommend you keep the chorus lyric really simple and repetitive, and save most of the details for the verses.

As a quick reminder, 'G/B' means a G chord over a B bass. Write a bridge today if you like, but you'll need to add your own chords.

[DAYS 5–6]
TITLE STARTER

[DAYS 5-6]

TITLE STARTER

"Suffer the pain of discipline or suffer the pain of regret."
ANONYMOUS

Another great way into a song is a title. Most of the time, a song's title is also its lyrical hook – the key word or phrase that's repeated a lot in the song's lyric. And as you might know, a good title captures your song's central idea in a direct, succinct and interesting way.

In fact, one hallmark of great songwriting is where every line in a song repeats, explores or expands on the song's title – or at least its big idea – in some way.

That means the trick with starting with a title is making sure your song's idea and title fit each other well, then building a lyric around that idea and title. That's what you're going to practice doing in this challenge.

Why it matters: A great song is organized around a great title – not only to capture your listener's attention but also to give you a single focus to craft a song about.

DAYS 5–6 CHALLENGE

 60–90 mins

Write a song using one of the following titles:

[1] **Enough**

[2] **Hasta Mañana**

[3] **Look But Don't Touch**

[4] **Too Late Now**

[5] **One More Time**

[6] **Class**

[7] **Patience**

If you want to, you can make changes to the title you've chosen – especially if it helps you integrate it within your chorus lyric.

Start wherever you like, but after you've figured out your song's central idea, story or message, it's a good idea to try write a chorus lyric that hammers your song's big idea home and includes the title somewhere, maybe more than once.

From there you might play around with finding instrumental grooves that also support your song's big idea – if it's a song with an upbeat message, you probably want an upbeat groove, for example – and add verses that expand on, explore and add detail to your song's overall message.

[DAYS 7–8]
FORBIDDEN LOVE

[DAYS 7–8]

FORBIDDEN LOVE

"Do what you can with all you have, wherever you are."
THEODORE ROOSEVELT

Sometimes, the trick to creating something remarkable is to give yourself a specific limitation or restriction. Creativity thrives on limitations, so paradoxical as it might sound, challenging yourself to work around a particular restriction can be a great way of motivating yourself to create something really original.

In today's challenge, you're going to write a really common song type – a love song – given one specific constraint.

Why it matters: If you want to create differently, you have to think differently. One great way of doing that is by giving yourself a specific restriction or limitation, then seeing what creative ideas it leads you to.

DAYS 7–8 CHALLENGE

 60–90 mins

Write a love song that never uses the word 'love'.

The trick here is coming up with an interesting and convincing way of saying 'I love you' without actually saying 'I love you'.

As always, try to figure out your song's big idea – who is singing, who is being sung to and what your song's main message is – before you begin. Whatever way you decide to say 'I love you' without using the word 'love' may also become your song's lyrical hook.

If you've written a similar song before, or you just fancy taking on an even tougher challenge, you can write a love song that never uses the word 'you' instead.

[DAYS 9–10]
WORD CLUSTER #1

[DAYS 9–10]

WORD CLUSTER #1

"The way to get started is to quit talking and begin doing."

WALT DISNEY

One really powerful way of getting your ideas flowing is to lower your standards and get down whatever ideas you have, as they come – because you can improve a bad idea but you can't improve no idea.

That means that early on in the creative process, the more ideas you can get down, the better. From there you'll usually find your mind picks out the most interesting ideas and starts joining them together – making the connections that you're going to use to build a complete song.

Today's challenge is about putting this idea into practice – I've given you a handful of words to play with and it's up to you to find connections between them and transform them into a lyric.

Why it matters: Songwriting is about forming connections between different ideas. Sometimes a great way to start a song is by sketching out words, phrases or musical ideas then figuring out how to connect them.

DAYS 9–10 CHALLENGE

 60–90 mins

Write a song that uses at least five of the words in this word cluster:

belong

see   devotion

truth   attitude   forever

loving   something

never   knowing

all

Which five? See which words jump out at you – and which start joining together to suggest some bigger situation or song idea.

Don't worry if that process takes a while – as always, it's important to have a strong song idea to work with. So don't be afraid to spend a good chunk of time making those decisions before you begin the actual writing.

One of these words could be part of your song's lyrical hook, or not. That's up to you. Just see what words your mind connects and see if you can follow where those connections take you. (And of course, if you end up using more than five of the words you get bonus points.)

[DAYS 11–12]
OFF THE HOOK

[DAYS 11–12]

OFF THE HOOK

"Whether you think you can or whether you think you can't,
you're right."
HENRY FORD

One simple but really effective way to write songs quickly is to make bold use of repetition – and especially in its chorus.

Obviously there's a point when repetition can get too much – and repetitive in the bad sense – but tasteful repetition is an important part of songwriting in every genre. In fact, sometimes – in songs ranging from Queen's 'We Will Rock You' to Ariana Grande's 'thank u, next' – you find choruses that are pretty much just the song's title repeated over and over.

Today you're going to practice using this technique in a song of your own.

Why it matters: Artful repetition is one of the cornerstones of good songwriting – and taking advantage of that can help you write high-quality songs more quickly.

DAYS 11–12 CHALLENGE

 60–90 mins

Write a song where the chorus features plenty of repetition of one or more hooks.

We've already talked about lyrical hooks, but you can create hooks from pretty much any part of your song – your vocal melody, your instrumental grooves, your lyric – anything you can repeat over and over again to 'hook' your listener in.

Maybe start by trying to find either a specific word or phrase – like 'Yeah' or 'No way' or 'What comes around goes around' – that sounds good sung over and over again. Or try finding some kind of interesting musical figure to loop – a fragment of a vocal melody, an instrumental idea, a drum beat, anything. Then try to build a chorus around that core repetition, bearing in mind you can tweak or edit the repeating figure as your song goes on, if you want to.

As I said, there's a point where repetition gets boring, but a lot of songwriters are surprised by how much you can repeat an idea before that happens. So lean into seeing how catchy and repetitive you can make your chorus – and how simply and quickly you can put it together.

Once you have your chorus, you can start building the rest of the song from there – clarifying exactly what the song's story or situation is, what the verses will say and sound like, and deciding whether you want to add a bridge, intro, outro or anything else. But whatever you do, concentrate first on finding that ultra-catchy and simple chorus, and building the rest of your song around it.

[DAYS 13–14]
ONE-TO-ONE

[DAYS 13–14]

ONE-TO-ONE

"The best way in the world for breaking up a writer's block
is to write a lot."
JOHN GARDNER

One of the most compelling types of song is a direct address song –
where the person singing says something directly to someone else.
This includes songs where people break up, songs where someone
confronts someone else about something, songs where someone
tells someone they're attracted to them – plus all kinds of other one-
to-one situations.

Given this format tends to produce really attention-grabbing
songs, it's exactly what you're going to practice writing today.

Why it matters: Songs tell stories, and the best stories
are usually dramatic. Being able to write songs that
address someone frankly and directly is an important
technique for writing attention-grabbing material.

DAYS 13–14 CHALLENGE

 60–90 mins

Write a compelling direct address song, sung by one particular person to another.

Maybe it's a breakup or a confrontation or a long-overdue chance to set the record straight with someone. Or maybe it's something more positive – a song where your singer says something kind that should have been said a long time ago. Just try to settle on a situation that seems compelling or dramatic to you and be really clear about who the two people involved in the song are – who's the song to and who's singing – and what kind of relationship there is between them.

From there, think about building a chorus that explores your song's idea in a direct way – and choosing a lyrical hook (or title) that expresses that. Then think about how you're going to set that idea up in the verses – what is the situation or story that has led up to the singer having to say what they have to say?

This song could be based on a real-life situation, or you could invent something. Either way, this challenge is a good opportunity to draw on your personal experiences of conflict or having frank conversations with people, and to inject all of that real-life experience into what you write.

[DAYS 15–16]
GET HAPPY

[DAYS 15–16]

GET HAPPY

"Most songs I write are spur-of-the-moment-type things.
I have to be spontaneous. If not, songwriting can bore me.
You can't over-think songs. You just can't."
ANTHONY HAMILTON

Songs sink or swim on the emotions they communicate. Songwriting isn't about crafting the smartest or most intricate music and lyrics – for your song to have impact, it just has to make people *feel* something.

At the same time, it's no secret that positive, uplifting music paired with a positive, uplifting message tends to be a great recipe for writing appealing songs. There's definitely an art to crafting a two- to four-minute song that focuses on a single, simple emotion in that way – and that's what you're going to practice today.

Why it matters: Sometimes the creative process gets messy and complicated, but your goal as a songwriter is always simplicity – especially in the emotion or mood that's at the heart of each song.

DAYS 15–16 CHALLENGE

 60–90 mins

Write a happy song.

Come up with any song idea or concept you like – a song about a particularly uplifting situation or story, a song that encourages people to smile more, a song about something positive that turned your life around.

It could even be something negative or unpleasant that you've put a positive spin on – how you learned to heal from a break-up or bereavement, how to deal with depression and anxiety, how to practice self-care when life gets tough – anything you like.

Just try to find a simple but decisive idea with an overall positive message, then try to turn that into a song that has a mood-lifting effect on its audience.

[DAY 17−18]
WORD CLUSTER #2

[DAYS 17–18]

WORD CLUSTER #2

"One of the nice things about songwriting is you can be
inspired by absolutely anything."
JENS LEKMAN

Writing songs – like most kinds of creativity – is a really intuitive process. Your subconscious is always connecting ideas in ways your conscious brain can't always recognize or explain.

That means a big part of your job as a songwriter is to trust your intuition to work its magic, even If you don't understand what that magic is yet. (That's another good reason to have faith in whatever ideas come to you – because they're often better and smarter than your conscious brain realizes.)

Today's word cluster is another chance to put that idea into practice. You'll get sixteen words this time, and the opportunity to let your intuition have fun making connections between them.

> **Why it matters:** Your subconscious is really good at making connections and creating order out of randomness, so learning to trust it to do its thing is a crucial part of the creative process.

DAYS 17–18 CHALLENGE

 **60–90 mins**

Write a song that uses at least five of the words in this word cluster:

show

never   before

pain   missing   late

burning   after   apology   fire

addiction   warning   let

insecure   pleasure

what

Your challenge today is exactly the same as on Days 9 and 10: look at the words above and see what they inspire in you, which ones seem to connect together, then start building a song out of those words and connections.

Again, try focusing on the song idea, story or situation the words inspire, and take things from there. And again, your goal is to use a minimum of five words from the cluster, but you can always use more if you like.

[DAYS 19–20]
THIS TIME IT'S
PERSONAL

[DAYS 19–20]

THIS TIME IT'S PERSONAL

"Have the courage to follow your heart and intuition. They
somehow already know what you truly want to become.
Everything else is secondary."
STEVE JOBS

On Days 13 and 14, we touched on the idea of using your personal experiences in what you write. And in a sense, every song you write is personal because it's informed by your experiences, beliefs and unique perspective on the world. That's what makes songwriting so interesting.

Your challenge today is about connecting with your personal experiences – and the things that make you unique – more directly. It's no secret that songwriting is a great medium for documenting real-life perspectives or real-life events – and that's what you're going to have a go at today.

Why it matters: Being able to draw directly on your personal experiences and perspectives in what you write is an essential songwriting tool.

DAYS 19–20 CHALLENGE

 60–90 mins

<u>Write a song from your perspective that is inspired directly from your personal experience or beliefs.</u>

There are lots of ways to do this, but let's assume this song is going to be sung by you. Whether you consider yourself a singer or not, write as yourself, even if it'll be sung by someone else later.

For starters, think about a key message or idea you have to say. Do you want to tell the story of something particular that happened to you? Is there something specific you're burning to tell someone? Do you have a piece of advice you'd love to share with the world?

Whatever you decide, focus on writing a song that lets us into your truth, your worldview, your perspective – or at least two to four minutes of it.

Meanwhile, try to write music that fits or captures you, your personality and your message. Try to blend all of the parts of the song together in a way that gives us a glimpse of who you are, what you feel and something specific you have to say.

[DAY 21–22]
THE RESPONSE
CHALLENGE

[DAYS 21–22]

THE RESPONSE CHALLENGE

"You don't have to be great to start,
but you have to start to be great."
ZIG ZIGLAR

Art inspires art. Artists inspire artists. In fact, there are no truly original ideas or art – everything is somehow a mashup of existing ideas and art, only put together in new and exciting ways.

That means, as a songwriter, it's important to be aware of other works of art you can respond to or be inspired by. Because while you can't just take someone else's song, copy it and call it your own, you can be inspired by another song, you can use some of its ideas, add a healthy dose of your own ideas and style, then turn all of that into something new. Because that's how creativity works.

And that's what you'll practice doing today.

Why it matters: The art of making art is the art of drawing inspiration or influence from the things you love, but turning all of that into something new.

DAYS 21–22 CHALLENGE

 60–90 mins

Write a song that responds to an existing song.

You can interpret the word 'respond' however you like. One great way to do this is to write a song that responds to the message or idea of an existing song – so if the existing song features a singer who says 'You need to treat me better', you could write a song that answers 'Yes, you're right' or 'I'll treat you better if…'.

Another is to write a song that is your personal, creative response to a song you admire – you could write something inspired by the way that song sounds, or take some elements of that song and use them in your own song, or write an homage song in the style of an artist you particularly admire.

And if you were wondering: no one can copyright a concept or idea. As long as you don't directly copy substantial parts of an existing song's music or lyrics, you're free to be inspired or influenced by the big ideas that went into creating someone else's song.

So think of a song you know and love. See what ideas or concepts it opens up for you. Think about how what it says and how you – or the people involved in that song's message – could respond. Then use that to spark your own, original song.

[DAY 23–24]
THE BALLAD
CHALLENGE

[DAYS 23–24]

THE BALLAD CHALLENGE

"I teach songwriting a lot, and I always tell my students,
'You gotta write the little songs sometimes to get to the next
big song in the chute.' You gotta write 'em to get to it. You
never know what's going to be a little song or a big song."
MARY GAUTHIER

Songwriting is storytelling – that's how songs work. Whether the stories are simple, convoluted, literally true, fabricated or somewhere in between, virtually every song situation is based on story of some kind.

Some songs, though, are really direct in telling the story of some other person or an event – they're ballads, in the oldest sense of the word – and that's the type of song you're going to try writing today.

Why it matters: Songwriting is storytelling, and being able to write songs that tell direct third-person stories is a great way of developing your storytelling skills.

DAYS 23–24 CHALLENGE

 **60–90 mins**

<u>Write a third-person song that directly tells someone's story.</u>

There are two key parts to starting this challenge. The first – and most important – is deciding who to write about. It can be anyone you like: someone real, someone invented, someone you know personally, someone you know about but have never met. Just pick someone whose life and/or life story interests you.

The second – and also important – is choosing a narrator, the voice of the song. That's because, similar to what we talked about on Days 19–20, the perspective and worldview of the song's narrator is going to affect what the song says. Probably the simplest narrator choice is you, but it could be someone else if you prefer.

Having made those two key decisions, try to figure out what the central message or focus of the song could be, because that's likely to become the central idea of the chorus or refrain. In other words, if the person singing had to summarize what the song is about in a single word or phrase, what would that be? It could be something like 'She always knows' or 'He's a live wire' or 'We'll miss him'.

From there, try building that message into a chorus or refrain. Then for the song's verses, have a think about what details, events or anecdotes you could include to support the song's key message.

If you've never written a refrain form before and want to try, this challenge is a great opportunity. Try writing three verses (refrain forms have no chorus) of 8 lines, finishing with a two-line repeated refrain each time. (Check Appendix 2 for more pointers.)

[DAYS 25 – 26]
TITLE REMIX

[DAYS 25–26]

TITLE REMIX

"The secret of getting ahead is getting started.
The secret of getting started is breaking your complex,
overwhelming tasks into small manageable tasks,
then starting on the first one."
MARK TWAIN

On Days 21 and 22 you wrote a song that was directly inspired by another. Today you'll do something similar, but differently.

One thing that makes songwriting so interesting is the way small changes to a lyrical or musical idea can create a completely different effect. Think, for example, about the difference between a song called 'Moving Out' and a song called 'Moving On' or 'Moving Up'.

Today you're going to put that idea into practice by taking one small element of a song you know and admire and using it to create a completely different song.

Why it matters: Creativity is the art of the remix –
taking ideas and inspiration from the art you admire and
doing your own thing with them.

DAYS 25–26 CHALLENGE

 60–90 mins

Take the title of a song that already exists and use it to write a completely different song.

As you know, a solid song idea, situation or story is essential to writing a good song. But the key to this challenge is that any specific word or phrase in a title can be used to capture or express plenty of contrasting song ideas.

For example, there are literally dozens of well-known songs called 'Hello' or 'Without You' or 'Tonight' that are about completely different situations and even communicate completely different overall messages.

So have a go. Pick an existing song, take its title and use it in a new song that uses the title in a completely different way. Try thinking laterally with the title – see what other stories or situations it could describe – and then build a new song around whatever you come up with.

[DAYS 27–28]
THE FAREWELL
CHALLENGE

[DAYS 27–28]

THE FAREWELL CHALLENGE

"It's very helpful to start with something that's true.
Something simple and true, that has a lot of possibilities,
is a nice way to begin."
PAUL SIMON

The best song ideas pull off two particular things at once. On the one hand, they're really universal – they're about ideas and situations that most people can empathize with. But on the other, they're really specific – they're about a particular situation that becomes an effective and specific representation of that larger idea.

Mastering this fundamental concept is what today's challenge is all about: tapping into the universal experience of saying farewell while finding a specific song idea that really brings that universal experience to life.

Why it matters: Great songwriting is a subtle blend of the universal – things anyone can relate to – and the specific – the details that create the specific world of your song.

DAYS 27–28 CHALLENGE

 **60–90 mins**

Write a farewell song.

Come up with any farewell song idea you like. It could be a straightforward goodbye, it could be a happy goodbye, it could be a bittersweet goodbye.

As I said, the key here is to look for a specific situation that also resonates universally – that relates somehow to situations lots of people have experienced.

From there, decide how you want to frame the song – is it a first- or third-person song? Then try and capture the specific kind of farewell you've chosen in the music and lyrics you create.

[DAYS 29–30]
SO MANY
POSSIBILITIES

[DAYS 29–30]

SO MANY POSSIBILITIES

"White. A blank page or canvas. His favorite.

So many possibilities."

JAMES LAPINE

Nice work – it's the final challenge. And your reward for getting this far is the chance to spend today writing anything you feel passionate about writing.

That's right – you get carte blanche to go wherever inspiration takes you. Is there a song you've always wanted to write? Was there a song idea you had in an earlier challenge but couldn't use? Is there a song idea that came to you just now? Well, go ahead. Today's your opportunity to make it happen.

> **Why it matters:** The best way to write your best songs is to write the songs you care about – you'll always do a better job when you're excited about what you're making.

DAYS 29–30 CHALLENGE

 **60–90 mins**

<u>Write any song you like, in any style you like, to any idea you like.</u>

You could use an idea you had but passed on in one of the earlier challenges. You could use an idea you've been interested in working with for a while. If that's not sparking anything, you could also leaf through the song prompts at the end of the book for inspiration.

But whatever you do, as usual, don't spend forever deciding on the perfect idea. Pick a simple and decisive idea and get writing. Take a shot on where that idea might take you and try things out – whatever comes – and enjoy letting those ideas take you wherever they're going to take you.

Good luck.

...AND BREATHE –
YOU DID IT!

...AND BREATHE – YOU DID IT!

Congratulations – you made it! You finished fifteen substantial songwriting challenges in thirty days, and no doubt finished them in style.

So take a bow. Pat yourself on the back. Celebrate with a beverage or two, if that's your thing. And take a couple of days off – you earned it.

But after you've done that, you might be wondering where to go next.

Well, first things first, if you saved everything you created during the fifteen challenges like I recommended, you'll have plenty of material to do something with. Maybe you're really proud of two or three of the songs you wrote, maybe eight or nine of them are OK, and maybe a couple are write-offs – but whatever the proportion, you won't be short of decent and even promising songs to play around with.

So dig them out and see what you could do with them. Some of the great songs might be more-or-less ready to go – to record, to perform live or to send on to a singer or artist you know is looking for new material.

As for the OK songs – or even a couple of the ones you're not so keen on – now is a great time to revisit them and see what you can improve or rewrite now that you have more time. As you know, your goal with these challenges was to write fifteen songs, not to write fifteen *perfect* songs. The truth is that plenty of great songs don't come out that great on the first draft, so now is a great time to dig up any material you think has unfulfilled potential and start reworking it – now you have as much time as you to need – to see where else you can take it.

Other than that, you know the drill: keep writing.

Keeping coming up with new material. If you're looking for new songwriting ideas, at the end of the book I've reproduced my list of *107 Song Prompts for When You're Really Stuck*. And for some more in-depth but diverse song prompts, there's my book *The Ultimate Book of Song Starters*, which contains 501 powerful but varied songwriting ideas and starting points for writing songs in any style or genre.

Alternatively, you could check out one of my other 30-Day Challenges, though in comparison to this one, you'll probably find them a walk in the park. You could also go back and try some of the challenges from a different angle – in a different style, with a different co-writer, with a totally different idea – if you like.

Whatever you decide, now is a great moment to look back on the amazing feat you just accomplished. Plenty of writers don't finish fifteen songs in a year, never mind in a month.

And most of all – you've proved to yourself how much you can write and how quickly you can write, when you set your mind to it, and that's going to help you create everything you create from here be all the more electric.

So congratulations. And happy creating, whatever's next for you.

ALSO BY ED BELL: *THE ART OF SONGWRITING*

The Art of Songwriting is a unique songwriting guide that's not about learning rules and following methods, but about **how to think, create and live like a songwriter**.

It covers all the big concepts that go into making great songs – not just the craft of songwriting, but how creativity works and what it means to be an artist.

The Art of Songwriting is available as an eBook at **thesongfoundry.com/ebook** and in paperback online and in bookstores.

[CODA]
FIVE SUREFIRE
WAYS OF BEATING
W****R'S B***K

[CODA]

FIVE SUREFIRE WAYS OF BEATING W****R'S B***K

The not-so-great news is that everyone feels creatively stuck or blocked sometimes, no matter how experienced they are. The most exciting thing about creativity is that it's wild and unpredictable – because that's how exciting new things are made – but that can be the most frustrating thing about it too.

But the good news is that there are plenty of specific, practical things you can do to fight w****r's b***k. And the great news is that experiencing w****r's b***k nearly always says more about your attitude towards being creative than your actual ability to create. So if you change your mind and change your attitude, you might just unlock a ton of creativity you didn't know you had inside.

Let's talk about five ways to do that – both within the fifteen challenges in this book and in everything else you create.

1. LOWER YOUR STANDARDS

I know. I get it. You want everything you write to be the best thing ever. You want every note and every word to touch hearts, change lives and wow literally everyone who hears them. You wish you had a creative Midas touch that could turn every song you ever touched into gold – no exceptions.

Because, honestly, most songwriters – myself included – feel like that sometimes. And that's not necessarily bad or wrong.

We want all those things because we have standards, we have values, we have taste – and that's a good thing. No, a great thing.

But the trouble is, creativity doesn't work like that.

99% of the time, creative ideas don't come out perfect the first time. They come out messy and wild and disorganized, and it's your job as an artist to organize, edit and polish those ideas until they come as close to perfect as you can get them.

More often than not, you have to write the bad, half-assed version before you can write the good, fully-assed version. The only way to find out which things do work is to try tons of things that don't. It's a gauntlet you have to pass through on each new creative project: try, fail, fail better, fail better until you succeed.

And that means if you're such a perfectionist you can't tolerate even one OK or average idea, you're not going to get very far as an artist. Sure, blank pages might look pretty, but they're nowhere near as fun as pages (or screens) with stuff on them. And pretty or not, you can't fix a blank page – though you can fix a page with average ideas on it.

So as weird and counterintuitive as it might sound, that means having too high standards early on in the creative process won't do you any favors. In fact, it's probably going to make things harder.

So next time you're feeling stuck or blocked, there's a simple way out of it: lower your standards, just for now. No one is ever truly blocked, everyone always has some kind of ideas – only, if you're in the habit of saying 'no, not good enough' to every idea you have, you'll end up feeling blocked pretty quickly.

If you can't seem to get any ideas down that you like, then don't. Get an idea down that you don't like. Then try to turn it into an idea you do like. Or try some other idea. And repeat.

There is a time and a place for high standards. That's later in the process. That's the stage when you've put plenty of ideas on the table and earned the privilege of picking out the most exciting ones and trying to polish them up into something really great.

But until you get there, the best thing you can do is keep your standards low and your mind open. You might miss a gem of an unpolished idea if you don't. Soon enough it'll be time to think about how to cut those gems so they really shine – but for now you've got to trust the process, compadre, and just get those ideas down.

2. START SIMPLE, START SMALL

There's a simple principle in art and in life which I guess you could call 'The Law of Getting Sh*t Done'. It goes like this:

Action – no matter how small – creates confidence.

Every failure to act – no matter how small – creates fear.

It's a spiral you're constantly going up or down in, all the time. Either you're doing things and gaining in confidence, or you're not doing things and losing confidence and letting fear creep in instead.

And the truth is, exactly what you do matters less than the fact that you do something – anything. By starting to act – by trying something – you start climbing up the spiral and gaining in confidence, which makes it easier to do more, which brings you more confidence, which makes it easier to do more, yada, yada, yada. And all you have to do is start.

So if you're feeling stuck or blocked, give yourself permission to start simple, start small. Maybe you don't know what your song's entire groove is going to sound like, but you could start by trying out a rhythm or four chords or a particular synth sound. Maybe you don't know what your song's entire lyric will be like, but you could start by trying out different titles. And maybe, just maybe, before you do any of those things it's worth taking a step back and figuring out, you know, what your song is even about in the first place.

Nobody's first word is 'monokerophobia'. Nobody learns to high jump before they learn to walk. And your next song is the same – sometimes you can't write the part you want to write until you've done the groundwork you have to do to be able to write it. Sometimes you're just not ready to create the part you want to create, so you have to create some other part first.

So give yourself permission to take the path of least resistance, whatever that may be. Give yourself permission to trust the process. Give yourself permission to accept that songwriting is hard. Then give your song permission to evolve step by step, idea by idea and even word by word or chord by chord.

One great way to put this into practice – especially if you're feeling really stuck – is to promise yourself you'll just write for 20 minutes without giving up, no matter what.

The first ten minutes might feel like agony, but – as you know – lower your standards and get some ideas down anyway.

Then, usually somewhere around minute 12 or 14, chances are you'll come up with something that excites you, just enough. It might not knock your socks off, it might not be perfect or polished, but it'll excite you, just enough. It'll capture your attention and maybe your imagination, just enough.

So you'll play around with it. You'll try to perfect or polish it. And then you'll keep playing around with it, or play around with one of the ideas it leads to. Then soon enough you're 20 minutes in, having completely forgotten about all that resistance you were feeling *less than half an hour ago*.

Another great technique when you're working on a project over a few days or a month is to intentionally leave yourself something simple and small to do first when you come back to write – something you know isn't going to give you a headache when you pick things up again. That way, it'll be much easier to slide back into writing and hit the ground running.

But whatever you do, remember the principle: it's better to take one tiny step than to stay exactly where you are. That's how you build your creative confidence and how you get moving on any creative project.

Make some bold, decisive choices – no matter how simple or how small – and see where they take you. If you don't like the way those choices turn out, just go back and try some different ones.

Then, in a nutshell, just keep doing that until your song is done, and *voilà* – where there once was w****r's b***k, there's now a song instead. All because you started somewhere – even somewhere super simple, or super small.

3. LET YOUR CURIOSITY LEAD THE WAY

There are tons of great things about being an artist, but one of the best is that you get to be curious – about everything and about everyone. You get to wonder about things, you get to want to know about things, you get to want to try things, read things, touch things, visit things, taste things and/or any combination of the above.

We've already talked about how having too high standards early on in the creative process won't do you any favors. But another important way to give each project the time and space it needs to develop is to make sure you don't have too narrow expectations about where it could or should go.

That might sound like heresy – you create something because you have a vision of what you want it to be. But sometimes, you try creating what you think you want something to be, but something else – maybe something equally as good, or even better – comes out instead. And it's important to be open to that possibility.

That's why a lot of creative people talk about trusting the process and trying to enjoy the ride, not focusing on the destination. Because the less you worry about arriving at some predetermined destination and the more you focus on doing what you can do right here, right now to move one step closer to somewhere exciting, the more fun you'll have and the more exciting things you'll create.

Or, to put it more simply, the best way to create is to let your curiosity – and not your expectations – lead the way.

Creativity is about letting go. It's about accepting what in front of you. It's about creating the things you can create even when they're not exactly the things you wanted to create.

When you were a kid, you didn't care exactly how your sandcastle was going to turn out or whether this afternoon's finger painting would be your masterpiece. You just got out your bucket and spade or stuck your hands in the paint tray and started making stuff. The more you can reconnect with that childlike curiosity and just see where each new creative project takes you – yes, that way round – the happier and more creative you'll be.

4. FIND A CREATIVE RITUAL OR PROCESS YOU CAN RELY ON

Sometimes the best thing you can do before you start is to tidy your workspace or wash the dishes or water your pet cacti, whatever you're into. Doing something repetitive and even mindless like that is a great way of clearing your mind of all the other crazy ish it's mulling over right now, and preparing yourself – in a world of pop-up ads, viral memes and smartphone notifications all fighting for your attention – to focus on what's in front of you. (Or on what you're about to create in front of you.)

Creativity thrives on the unexpected – but you don't have to. If you want to write in a different space every day, then do. But if settling into your workspace, drinking a particular flavor of coffee, or taking a walk round your neighborhood is part of what you do to tell your brain it's time to sit down and create, then great. Go for it.

And sure, maybe that sounds boring. Maybe it's not the crazy rockstar vision of being a songwriter you imagined. But it's the real-life reality of what you sometimes have to do to get new work done.

And as for process – as I say in *The Art of Songwriting*, part of the thrill of writing is that every new song has its own process. It's OK to have go-to methods or starting points if they work for you though. If you like to start with titles, start with titles. If you like to start with grooves, start with grooves. If you have particular sources of inspiration, ideas and/or motivation you like to use, use them.

Again, find the path of least resistance – for you and this project – in whatever you do, and don't be embarrassed about falling back on a regular habit or process if it makes creating new things easier for you.

5. TRY TO CONNECT WITH 'WHY?'

In *The Ultimate Book of Song Starters* I talk about how 'what if?' is the question that drives creative projects forward. But the question that best drives creative people forward is 'why?'.

Like, why should this project exist? Why do you care about creating it? Why does the world need to see or hear it?

Sometimes when it comes to creating something new, it's easy to get knee-deep in the details of the thing and forget why you're creating the thing in the first place. Maybe it's to share a particular message. Maybe it's to make people feel something. Maybe it's to share something you think is important with the world.

Whatever your 'why?' is, try to keep it in mind while you write. Better yet, put it on a piece of paper and stick it somewhere above your workspace so you can't forget it.

That usually causes two powerful and exciting things to happen.

One: it'll remind you why you're writing, what you're ultimately trying to do, and why – even when things get difficult – it'll all be worth the effort.

And two: it'll help you sweat the details less and focus on your bigger purpose or vision more. You're less likely to sweat the little details the more you keep the big picture in mind. And having a bigger purpose or vision to measure your ideas against is a great way of figuring out which ideas should and shouldn't belong in this song.

That's not to say, of course, that the details don't matter. They do. But the details don't matter – and often don't work – unless they're working together to add up to some bigger vision or purpose. So the more you connect with *why* you're creating what you're creating – no matter how simple that reason might be – the easier it is to create it.

* * *

For more resources on creativity and all areas of songwriting both in theory and in practice, I keep a comprehensive reading list on The Song Foundry site at **thesongfoundry.com/bookshelf**.

But if you're looking for an instant creativity hit, two great places to start are Steven Pressfield's classic *The War of Art* and Austin Kleon's *Steal Like an Artist*. There's also plenty more practical advice about how to improve your songwriting process and unlock your creativity in my book *The Art of Songwriting*.

[APPENDIXES]

[APPENDIX 1]

SONG STRUCTURE CHEATSHEET

If you've been writing a while, you'll know the main song forms pretty well. But if you need a reminder, or want to brush up on your songwriting theory, here's a quick summary of the two main song forms I suggest you use throughout these challenges.

VERSE-CHORUS STRUCTURE

Verse-chorus structures rely on two sections that work together to create a particular rise-and-fall cycle: the verse and chorus.

In general, the job of the verses is to introduce and set up the context, situation or story of the song, while the job of the chorus is to repeat the central idea of the song over and over again in the most direct way.

All of the choruses are usually identical melodically and lyrically, while the verses are usually the same melodically (more or less) but with new lyrics each time.

Musically, a song's choruses are also almost always at a higher intensity or energy level than its verses. The verses often start building somewhere in their second halves in anticipation of the moment the next chorus arrives.

If you add a bridge, it usually comes after the second chorus, and takes us somewhere completely fresh musically and lyrically.

For simplicity, throughout the challenges I recommend you stick to these two archetypal versions of the form and keep each section eight lines and 16 measures long:

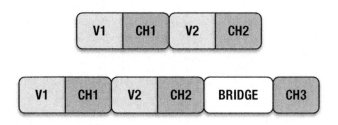

REFRAIN FORM

Refrain forms have one central section – also called a verse – where the last two lines (or occasionally just one) are the same each time. These lines are called the refrain, and function as a kind of mini chorus.

Generally in a refrain form, the melody of each verse is identical but the lyric – except for the refrain – is fresh each time.

Honestly, the vast majority of songs being written today are verse-chorus structures, so if you decide to write fifteen verse-chorus songs in this challenge, that's absolutely fine. But if you want to mix things up, you can try writing a refrain form – of probably two or three verses.

If you do, I recommend you make each verse eight lines long with a one- or two-line refrain. That will probably correspond to sixteen measures of music, or just eight if the tempo is particularly slow.

[APPENDIX 2]

ONE EFFECTIVE SONGWRITING PROCESS

There are *tons* of effective ways of writing songs – and most writers work in different ways depending on the song they're writing and the material they start with.

But in case it's useful, here's one particular step-by-step process – based on the process I outline in my book *How to Write a Song (Even If You've Never Written One Before and You Think You Suck)* – that is an effective way of tackling the challenges in this book.

[1] Find a song idea

Figure out who is singing, who they're singing to and what they're trying to say. That's a really important step before you make firm decisions on anything else.

[2] Find a lyrical hook (or title)

Pick a good lyrical hook – a word or phrase that neatly captures your song idea. (The lyrical hook is usually also the song's title.)

[3] Write the chorus

Write a chorus lyric that features the lyrical hook in a prominent way – and often more than once. Write the chorus chords, melody and groove in whatever order they come most easily.

[4] Write the first verse

Start building a verse lyric that sets up your chorus, and write the chords, melody and groove in whatever order they come most easily.

[5] Write the second verse

Try and find a new angle for the second verse: a different focus, something chronologically later, a different topic. Then write a new verse lyric, keeping the first verse chords, melody and groove more or less intact.

[6] Add a bridge if you like

Take us somewhere that feels fresh or like a diversion with the bridge lyric, chords, melody and groove.

[7] Add an intro and outro, plus any transitional sections in the main body of the song if you like

The intro can be as simple as a pre-extension of first verse groove. The outro can be as simple as an extension of the final chorus (or a repeat and fade). You could also add a short transitional section – sometimes called a turnaround – after your choruses to give your audience and singer a breather.

[APPENDIX 3]

107 BONUS SONG PROMPTS

If you're looking for more song ideas, here are a ton of them from one of my most popular articles on The Song Foundry site, *107 Song Prompts for When You're Really Stuck.* (You might recognize a couple that I adapted to create the challenges in this book.)

As you'll know if you've read the article — 30-day challenges aside, I have mixed feelings about song prompts. On the one hand, I think it's really important for you to be able to come up with and be excited about your own song ideas, not just the ideas someone else put in front of you. But on the other, I know that sometimes being given a specific idea or prompt can be the ticket to an exciting song you'd maybe never have written on your own.

So here we are — 107 quick song prompts that might inspire or challenge you to create something amazing you might not have thought of otherwise.

Finally, if you're looking for even *more* song ideas and inspiration, you'll probably enjoy my book *The Ultimate Book of Song Starters: 501 Powerful and Creative Ideas for Writing New Songs* — which contains exactly that many song prompts as well as plenty of ideas and advice about how to use them effectively.

Happy writing.

LOVE SONGS

---

1.   Write a love song. Any love song.

2.   Write a love song from you to a current or former lover.

3.   Write a love song from you to a desired or imaginary lover.

4.   Write a love song from someone else to his or her lover.

5.   Write a love song about an unusual kind of love.

6.   Write a love song about a complicated kind of love.

7.   Write a love song that never uses the word 'love'.

8.   Write a love song that never uses the word 'you'.

BREAK UP SONGS

9. Write a song where you break up with someone and you're really happy about it.

10. Write a song where you break up with someone and you're really sad about it.

11. Write a song where you break up with someone and you're conflicted about it.

12. Write a song where you break up with someone but you're terrified of doing it.

13. Write a song where you break up with someone suddenly after learning something new.

14. Write a song where someone broke up with you and you want them back.

15. Write a song where someone broke up with you and don't want them back.

16. Write a song where someone broke up with you and you're not sure if you want them back.

RELATIONSHIP SONGS

17. Write a song that says 'I've never met anyone like you before.'

18. Write a song that says 'Show me some respect.'

19. Write a song that says 'I don't care.'

20. Write a song that says 'I don't want to know.'

21. Write a song that asks 'Baby, what's wrong?'

22. Write a song that says hello.

23. Write a song that says goodbye.

STORY SONGS

24. Write a song that tells the story of someone you think is really interesting.

25. Write a song that tells the story of someone you think is misunderstood.

26. Write a song that tells the story of someone you really dislike.

27. Write a song that tells the story of someone you know personally.

28. Write a song that tells the story of someone you read about in the news.

29. Write a song that tells the story of an existing fictional character.

30. Write a song that tells a story about you, but from someone else's perspective.

PERSONAL / ARTIST SONGS

31. Write a song that introduces us to you as an artist.

32. Write a song that introduces us to someone else as an artist.

33. Write a song based on your key life philosophy.

34. Write a song that tells us something nobody else knows about you.

35. Write a song about a major event in your life.

36. Write a song about a major change in your life.

37. Write a song about what you want in life.

38. Write a song about your biggest hope in life.

39. Write a song about your biggest disappointment in life.

40. Write a song about growing up in your particular neighborhood.

I AM SONGS

41. Write a song that says 'I'm happy.' (And tell us why.)

42. Write a song that says 'I'm sad.' (And tell us why.)

43. Write a song that says 'I don't know.'

44. Write a song that says 'Nothing's gonna stop me.'

45. Write a song that says 'Something awesome is coming.'

46. Write a song that says 'I've been holding myself back all this time.'

47. Write a song that says 'I'm ready to start a new chapter in my life.'

48. Write a song that says 'I need help.'

49. Write a song that says 'I never saw that coming.'

50. Write a song that says 'I was right all along.'

PUBLIC SERVICE ANNOUNCEMENT SONGS

51.   Write a song that makes people feel happy.

52.   Write a song that makes people laugh.

53.   Write a song that makes people want to dance.

54.   Write a song that makes people say 'I love you' more.

55.   Write a song that motivates people.

56.   Write a song that encourages people to be themselves.

57.   Write a PSA (public service announcement) song of your choice – think 'Always Wear Sunscreen'.

OTHER STORY SONGS

58. Write a song from a parent to their son or daughter.

59. Write a song from a son or daughter to their parent.

60. Write a song for two friends.

61. Write a song for two enemies.

62. Write a song for two siblings.

63. Write a song for two lovers.

64. Write a song about getting married.

65. Write a song about eloping.

66. Write a song about moving to a new town.

67. Write a Christmas song.

68. Write a Hanukkah song.

69. Write a song for Hallowe'en.

70. Write a song for summer.

71. Write a 'We make a great team' song.

72. Write a 'What would I do without you?' song.

START WITH A LYRICAL HOOK (TITLE)

73. Write a song with a one-word lyrical hook – think 'Jealousy', 'Hello', 'Fever'.

74. Write a song with a two-word lyrical hook – think 'Bad Romance', 'Space Cowboy'.

75. Write a song with a lyrical hook that's a phrase – think 'No Good at Goodbyes'.

76. Write a song with a lyrical hook that's a complete sentence – think 'I'm Outta Love'.

77. Write a song with a lyrical hook that's a question – think 'Where Is the Love?'.

78. Come up with a totally original word or phrase – think 'Love Foolosophy', 'Ghetto Gospel' – and make that your lyrical hook.

79. Take the lyrical hook of an existing song, change one word and make that your hook.

80. Take the lyrical hook of an existing song, make that your hook BUT write about a completely different story or situation.

START WITH A MELODY

81. Write a perky melody, figure out a song story that fits it, then write that song.

82. Write a simple melody, figure out a song story that fits it, then write that song.

83. Write an expressive melody, figure out a song story that fits it, then write that song.

84. Write a melancholy melody, figure out a song story that fits it, then write that song.

85. Write a melody that repeats a single rhythmic motif, figure out a song story that fits it, then write that song.

START WITH A GROOVE

86. Write an upbeat groove, figure out a song story that fits it, then write that song.

87. Write a melancholy groove, figure out a song story that fits it, then write that song.

88. Write a funky groove, figure out a song story that fits it, then write that song.

89. Write a weird-sounding groove, figure out a song story that fits it, then write that song.

90. Write a chilled-out groove, figure out a song story that fits it, then write that song.

91. Write a groove based on two alternating chords, figure out a song story that fits it, then write that song.

92. Write a groove based on a simple three- or four-chord progression, figure out a song story that fits it, then write that song.

93. Write a groove based on a chord progression from an existing song, figure out a song story that fits it, then write that song.

94. Set a drum loop playing then freestyle lyrics over the top until that gives you a song idea. Then write that song.

MISCELLANEOUS

95. Write a song about life on other planets.

96. Write a song about your pet rock Ignacio.

97. Write a song about the Northern Line Extension to Battersea.

98. Write a song about the life and death of Hildegard von Bingen.

99. Write a song about a sweet potato that looks like Michael Caine.

100. Write a song that never uses the letter 'm'.

101. Write a song that has a 60-second sackbut solo.

102. Write the song you've always wanted to write.

103. Write the song you've just decided you wanted to write.

104. Write the song you've never wanted to write.

105. Write the song you still don't want to write.

106. Write the song you're totally petrified to write.

107. Just write something. Anything. Anything you like.

For more tools, ideas and inspiration,
visit **thesongfoundry.com**

Printed in Great Britain
by Amazon